Never Let a Skinny Guy Make Sandwiches

By GENE MUELLER and BOB DENYER

A HILARIOUS COLLECTION OF FISHING AND HUNTING TALES, SPICED WITH SOUND ADVICE AND USEABLE TIPS FROM TWO WACKY OUTDOORSMEN.

THIS BOOK IS DEDICATED TO LINDA MUELLER AND MARIA DENYER, TWO VERY PATIENT WIVES WHO HAVE BEEN STEADFAST IN THEIR SUPPORT OVER THE YEARS.

Thank you!

Gene and Bob

Charles County, Md., 1993

Our deepest gratitude and appreciation go to Bill Garner without whose help this book would have turned out to be nothing more than type-filled pages. Bill made sure that didn't happen. We'll never forget his generosity.

INTRODUCTION

Ideas for books often are rooted in strange and fascinating places. Among the giants of literature, for example, Ernest Hemingway's efforts frequently were driven by events that occurred during the deadly Spanish civil war, or the time spent in bullfighting corridas, or aboard Cuban billfishing boats. High drama sometimes spawns great books. However, the super-stars of literature universally have one shortcoming: they forget what regular, everyday people do with their lives because they don't live like everyday people.

Never fear! The authors of "Never Let A Skinny Guy Make Sandwiches" have little in common with Papa Hemingway and other great writers. Sure, they enjoy writing and they like to fish and hunt and enjoy a good drink at the end of a satisfying day afield, but that's where all similarities end. Inside the book you'll see a story that particularly addresses why people who like to eat should never allow a skinny person to volunteer to bring the sandwiches to an outing. In simple language, skinny folks more often than not wouldn't know good food from bad if their lives depended on it.

Meanwhile, the "Never Let A Skinny Guy Make Sandwiches" writers know a lot about eating and cooking. In addition, unlike Hemingway, they shave every day, have been married to their wives for many more years than Papa ever managed to stay hitched, and they've never been to Idaho.

But most of all, they've never stopped loving life. Laughter, they believe, is indeed a very potent formula for staying healthy and optimistic in an increasingly dour world.

Gene Mueller
Bob Denyer

Charles County, Md.

INDEX

CHAPTER 1
First, You Must Learn About The Weather

How To Be Your Own Forecaster 5

Wild Turkeys In The Rain 9

It's Never Too Cold For The Chinaman 13

Hunting Guides Lie Like A Rug (And Fishing
Captains Aren't Much Better) 18

When Not to Worry About the Rain 24

CHAPTER 2
If You Can't Join 'em, Lick 'em!

The Yuppie Coon Hunting Club 25

Not All Jumpers Are Horses 28

The Strangest Dog Breeds Of All Time 32

Sparkle Boats Do Strange Things To Men 38

Duck, Bill, Duck! 42

Sometimes It's Smart To Be Dumb 45

Cops Know Nothing About Runaway Dogs 47

How to Fool Squirrels 48

CHAPTER 3
Food & Drink Are More Important Than Fish & Game

Never Let A Skinny Guy Make Sandwiches 49

Sausage Gravy Is Better Than Wheat Germ 54

Moonshine Isn't Always A Lunar Condition 59

A Good-time Lexicon For Outdoorsmen 63

Sure-Fire Way to Catch Trout Through Ice 66

Ginger's Recipe for Tender Venison 67

CHAPTER 1

First You Must Learn About The Weather

HOW TO BE YOUR OWN FORECASTER

You'll find that even the most learned person rarely knows much about the weather. This particularly includes the many television meteorologists who either have a strange sense of humor, or no sense of humor at all.

"Hey, (fill in the name of your city), today will be a great day. We'll have steady, fresh breezes that'll make you wish you were out on the water in your sailboat," the weather forecaster will say almost anywhere in the United States. You'll hear this silly stuff even in the middle of South Dakota where you could only sail a boat if it had rubber tires on it that can run across grass.

Weather people sometimes watch the flag on a pole sticking out straight as a ramrod and talk about how refreshing the wind will feel. To which we can only say, "No, you jerk, it won't be refreshing at all because we're fishermen who absolutely hate any kind of wind that is faster than 5 m.p.h."

Wind is the enemy of decent fishermen everywhere. Anglers depend on calm weather so they can hold their boats steady while making thousands of casts during the day. Accurate casting and holding the boat in one place is impossible when it howls out on the water. Even shoreline fishermen hate the wind because it tips over their plastic fast-food store coffee cups. Besides, what is it about sailing that elicits such enthusiasm from meteorologists? Of all the many millions of U.S. boaters, only 18 percent actually like to sail. Besides, where we live, in Chesapeake Bay country, the "baggy-wrinkle" set only hoists a sail when another sailboat approaches them.

When that happens, the four-flushing phony unfurls his nylon (canvas is passe) and pretends to be propelled by the wind. But when nobody is looking, most sailboaters putt-putt along, letting their Volvo inboard motors do all the work. In fact, we suspect that most sailboat owners don't even know how to sail. They'd much rather use a gasoline motor and to heck with "tacking against the wind." With a motor you don't have to "tack."

One thing is certain, when it blows there's precious little you can do about it. However, we're here to help you with certain facts of the stormy life some fishermen and hunters encounter throughout their lives.

How To Tell When It's Too Windy To Fish

Take a knitted cap of the type worn in open-air football stadiums during winter. Soak the wool cap in your sink. We mean, soak it! Don't mess around. You want at least five pounds of water in that cap.

Now put it on your head. Don't wring it out first. We want your head dripping with the water that's coming from the toboggan cap. Now go outside where it's blowing. If the wind knocks that cap from your noggin, it's too windy to be fishing. Stay indoors.

But if the cap stays on your head, go fishing, but keep close to the shore because it's a shorter walk to firm ground once your boat is swamped with water.

There's no need to thank us for this tip. That's what we're here for. That, and to tell you how to tell apart the various cloud formations that can seriously affect your day outdoors. Read on!

Learn To Read The Clouds

We've discovered over many years of suffering through various kinds of weather that there are only three types of clouds that play a role in your outdoors activities.

The first cloud formations you must learn about are the cirrus types. These are drawn-out, wispy stringbeans of clouds that mean absolutely nothing. If you see cirrus clouds, go ahead and do what you want. Cirrus clouds are wimps.

Then there are the cumulus clouds. Now, cumulus formations are the type copied for television advertisements by toilet paper companies. They're puffy, look soft and huggable, kind of like fat, happy babies. You want to squeeze one when you see it. Cumulus clouds generally mean that something will happen down the road, but not today. So go ahead and keep fishing, hunting, hiking, camping — whatever makes you happy.

The third cloud formation can only be described as follows: Great big black bastards. We call them GBBBs.

GBBBs can put a hurting on you. Gosh, can they ever! But for some reason we never hear weather forecasters talk about them. When you see a huge black cloud slide toward you while you're fishing, evacuate the area because in less time than you could spell thunder and lightning, you'll be in the middle of it. Being on the water during a lightning storm while great big black bastard clouds cluster all around you is definitely not recommended.

Mind you now, we're no chickens. But when the aforementioned clouds arrive — we depart!

WILD TURKEYS IN THE RAIN

No one really knows why anybody pays attention to a guy who only rarely hunts wild turkeys, but the day before a recent Maryland wild turkey spring hunting season began Bob called all his friends (he has two) and told them to meet at his house. "We'll go turkey shootin'," he said. "I have a place that's crawlin' with the critters. We'll be back home before 9 o'clock — that's how sure I am we'll each get a bird," he added.

The following morning — around the time when most suburban cops start looking for a quiet place behind the trash bins of a shopping center, where they can park their cruisers and not be discovered while they're sleeping — we met at Bob's house. A soft rain fell and no one was really concerned with it. "In fact, the rain will actually help us," said Bob, who remained cheerful and optimistic even as the precipitation increased tremendously as we drove along still deserted highways toward the northern parts of the state.

In a place called Thurmont, in Frederick County, where hardwood and pine forests meet rolling farmlands, Bob motioned to a small opening along the road where the pickup truck could be parked. The rain now cascaded over the windshield and the wipers couldn't keep up with the cleaning chores even when switched to high speed. We'll walk over to those pines," said Bob, "where it'll be dry as indoors. Those pines won't allow any rain to penetrate. I was in there last year when it rained and I was completely protected."

The first guy who stepped from the truck so he could get the rest of his clothing from inside the truck bed, which was protected by a small camper shell, stepped into roughly 18 inches of water. "Damn it all to hell," said the hunter who now had wet feet. "Why didn't you tell me you parked in a creek?" Bob only raised his shoulders a bit and said, "That's not a creek. Usually it's a dry spot." Bob wasn't even a little embarrassed.

The man who rode in the middle of the truck's bench seat now knew better, so he tried to clear the water-filled low spot next to the vehicle with a smartly executed jump from the truck's doorway. He slipped and fell. He now had a wet rump. "Jeeezus, I can't believe I'm here doing this," he mumbled in the dark.

Soon the three turkey hunters walked across what used to be a dry grassy field. Unfortunately, now it was soaked from the rain and every step forward became a minor triumph. The trio sank into muddy bogs, slipped and slid, cursed softly, but not one of the men would ever admit loudly that he'd rather be at home in bed with his wife.

"There we are," Bob finally whispered. "The pines. Let's go inside where we'll be comfortable."

"If the rain can't get through these pines, I guess I

must be sweating," said Bubba, one of Bob's best friends who saw rivulets of water pouring over his hat brim and now had serious thoughts about friendships and hunting trips. Bubba wanted to be in a breakfast restaurant ordering homefries, toast, sausage and three sunny-side-up eggs. He was ready to abandon the turkey outing, that much was sure.

"Psssst!" whispered Bob as a bit of daylight crept over the horizon. "I heard something. Could be turkeys are starting to leave their roosts. Be careful now. Let's spread out a bit and watch the hollow down in front of us. I saw them come through there last time I was here."

"Did it rain then?" asked Bubba. "No," said Bob quietly, "but these are wild birds who don't care about rain. They live with it." Bob's pal didn't have the heart to mention that wild turkeys weren't like wild geese and ducks whose feathers were saturated with water-repellent oils. Turkeys liked rain about as much as Bubba, whose stomach now started to rumble audibly.

"What was that?" Bob wanted to know suddenly when a distant, high-pitched noise could be heard. The third man in the party reached into his shoulder bag and pulled out a turkey calling box — a rectangular, hollow contraption with a moveable lid on top that would fairly copy a yelping hen turkey when the lid was struck across the edges of the box in short, smart moves.

"Yupp, yupp, yipp, yipp," said the box as the three

hunters listened intently for an answer that might give away a love-sick strutting gobbler.

"Yipp, yipp, yupp, yipp," the calling box beckoned again and from the foggy hollow, somewhere across the ridge where dim lights could be seen in the distance, came an answer.

"Cock-a-doodle-doo," shouted a rooster from a farmer's barn, where — no doubt about it — it was dry as a bone.

"Yeah, eggs and sausage sound pretty good right about now," said Bob, wiping the wetness from his face.

IT'S NEVER TOO COLD FOR THE CHINAMAN

Everybody who enjoys being outdoors has met people who like the invigorating scent of fresh air as much as anyone but, unfortunately, have a tough time dealing with the elements for one reason or another. Some simply can't abide bugs, others hate searing heat, and a few have never gotten used to extremely cold weather. It is those types of "outdoorsmen" to whom this story is dedicated because for them the going is never easy. Still, they persist and in the end become winners of a special kind.

Our friend Dean Lee is one of those people. While his ancestors came from China, rest assured that he's as American as apple pie. In fact, he served his Navy enlistment time on the aircraft carrier Forrestal. Can't get any more American than that, can you? And if anyone says that our calling him a "Chinaman" is insensitive, forget it. That term comes from Dean himself. Dean, who believes that some folks are simply too sensitive, doesn't like hyphenated ethnic tags, such as Chinese-American, African-American, Polish-American, and heaven only knows how many other kinds of Americans.

Dean loves to hunt and although we sometimes tell ourselves that the only reason he likes to hunt is to be with his friends that's really not true. Sure, he enjoys the company of good pals, but he'll also hunt by himself, often staying atop a deer hunting stand in a tree for many hours on end then driving home because his friends couldn't be with him that day. It should also be mentioned that he's bagged his share of white-tailed deer, rabbits, squirrels, and waterfowl and pheasants. In fact, he once shot a fine buck over 100 yards away with an authentic muzzleloading Pennsylvania mountain rifle that was well over 140 years old.

That out of the way, Dean must also be credited with being a loyal pal, and when his friends go hunting, it is not unusual for the Chinaman to leave his area early just so he can be back at the camp or the vehicles to heat up a pot of delectable fried rice with bits of wild goose cooked into it, or the remainder of a venison roast. There's absolutely nothing Dean will not do to please the people he loves and the good cheer he spreads is returned again and again.

But all good things must come to an end. In the case of the Chinaman this usually occurs when the mercury drops through a hole in the ground and it gets cold. We're talking so cold that if you spit, it lands in the form of an icicle. Now that's cold!

It is during such days when our bosom buddy really suffers. After all, some people can cope with cold and other can't. Dean copes, but he'd rather do his coping in Hawaii than in Greenland, especially when December and January roll around. You get the drift, I'm sure.

All this leads us to recall an unusually harsh November deer season in Maryland. It was cold enough to watch Dean arrive at our meeting place alongside a creek and the woods we were about to hunt in clad in four layers of prime Northern goose down clothing, double-insulated gloves, goose down-lined hat and a woolly scarf wrapped around his face as he steadily sipped scalding hot coffee. On occasion, he'd switch to pouring a strange brew of Chinese tea into a metal cup. The grey-looking liquid had the undesirable taste of unsweetened swamp water. And all this happened before he even got out of his vehicle.

About a half hour before daybreak, we'd leave our cars and trucks and quickly discuss who sat in what tree stand and always add the warning that anyone who'd leave his stand before 11 a.m. would be taken to the wood-shed for a real butt-kicking. Of course, the threats were never carried out, but the warning stuck. Our gang of hunters knew better than to waltz around in the woods simply because it got too cold while waiting for deer action high up in a tree.

Dean would stand there and listen and steadily nod his head. Then he'd disappear among the pines, oaks and hickories and the bull brambles that are typical of southern Maryland bottomlands. How he eventually climbed into his deer stand that was well concealed by dense holly trees and the other growth around him is anybody's guess, but he did. As the appointed time of 11 a.m. arrived, what with nothing that had antlers having shown up, one of Dean's friends couldn't stand staying in his own tree platform any longer and he climbed down, along the way hoping to do a little still-hunting, moving, stopping, looking slowly around, hoping to walk into a deer he could take a quick shot at. After all, during cold, gray, overcast days, the deer sometimes move about all day. That's when he saw it. There in the distance, no more than 150 yards away — just out of the sure-fire range of a 12-gauge shotgun that was loaded with rifled slugs — there stood a perfectly edible, legally huntable doe. (Most of the guys in our group have stopped hunting for only trophy deer long ago. These days, we'd rather have a doe in the freezer than a buck because the girl deer usually are more flavorful and tender. Besides, you can't eat antlers, so why bother?)

The large female grazed a bit, then started pecking away at fallen acorns. All that right in front of Dean's stand, but our loveable Chinaman didn't move. His gun lay cradled in his arms. His face stared straight ahead. He seemed oblivious to the goings-on beneath him, which seemed strange since he easily could have bagged himself at least 80 pounds of venison.

The other hunter honored Dean's area and never took a crack at the deer that eventually smelled a rat and disappeared in the dense vines and swampy terrain that is so typical of the Southern Maryland landscape.

Now, the hunter near Dean's stand approached and loudly whispered up toward the branches that supported a strong wooden platform, "Why didn't you shoot that doe?"

"Because I couldn't move, " Dean hissed back. Then he said what some of his friends suspected all along. "I've got too many clothes on," he whispered. "I couldn't move my arms up high enough to bring my gunsights in line with my eyes. Damn it all!" Then, in an afterthought, he added, "Can you climb up here and help me get some of these clothes off so I can get down? I'm dying to walk back to my car and have a hot cup of something."

The morale of that story is that it doesn't pay to dress like a mummy because your friends will think you're a dummy.

HUNTING GUIDES LIE LIKE A RUG
(AND FISHING CAPTAINS AREN'T MUCH BETTER)

If you're like most outdoors people you've probably had your share of experiences with hunting and fishing guides and outfitters. Here's hoping yours have been as good, generally, as ours have been.

But there is one problem that bothers us as concerns a fair number of hunting guides. Why do so many of them feel they have to lie like a rug when you engage their services in anticipation of a day of duck or goose shooting, a caribou stalk, or a ride in the sage brush to look for a couple of big antelope bucks?

Here's betting your nickel against a crisp $50 bill that almost every guide will use the weather to his advantage. It doesn't matter what kind of weather — just as long as it can be used.

Our favorite right after you've bagged a limit of Canada geese from an in-ground hiding spot that looks like a freshly-dug grave and is known as a goose pit, is, "See how quick that happened? It's the northeast wind. It'll bring those birds to the decoys every time!"

You sit there looking very much like one of those head-bobbing German shepherd figurines in the back window of old Chevrolets, and you believe every word the guy has just said.

The trouble is that the very next day, when a cash-carrying party of four is wiped out and skunked with nary a bird to show for the effort, the guide is prone to say, "See what I mean? It's that damned northeast wind. It'll do it to you every time."

And you? You nod and look like a head bobbing . . . . well, you already know the rest.

Fishing guides and charter fishing captains are no different. You've heard the worn-out, old line, "You should have been here yesterday." It's the dumbest thing the pay-us-to-fish people could possibly say. Imagine after having a really tough day and not hooking anything (or very little) and then hearing a boat captain say, "You should have been here yesterday." You'll want to strangle the man with an itchy lambswool scarf.

The fishing captains, just like their cousins the hunting guides, also play the weather to the max. We'll guarantee that if you have a great day of fishing in a river while the tide is up, the boat guide or captain sooner or later will mention something about the high tides being responsible for it. Conversely, if the fishing is lousy, you'll soon have him blaming the same high tide for the poor success.

By the way, if you spend much time with a charter captain, a fishing or a hunting outfitter, you'll soon discover they have a standard list of self-serving claims that'll be thrown at you to get you to believe you've chosen a particularly tough game or fish species to go after.

In the case of fishing, don't be surprised to hear a bass guide say that a largemouth is the toughest, meanest thing that lives in the water, or that a smallmouth bass is, "inch for inch, the fightingest critter in any river." Oh, yeah? As concerns the largemouth, sure it's strong and, yes, it knows its underwater home just like any other fish knows it. But in similar-looking terrain, even if it's in a mangrove root-filled saltwater environment, it can't compare to a snook. Not even a little bit. And a largemouth doesn't know what tough is when you match a ticked-off striper or a northern pike against it under the same circumstances.

As concerns a smallmouth, yes it's a fine river inhabitant that will delight anybody — including us. But to say that it's the toughest fighter in the world of fishing is like saying a bantamweight boxer could have taken on Muhammad Ali when "The Greatest" was in top form. No way! Compared to an Argentine dorado, or New Zealand's Niugini bass, all of whom swim around in freshwater rivers, the smallmouth bass is a lightweight.

Yet, American fishing guides continue to exaggerate their prey when it really isn't necessary. Sure, we understand why they do it, but it really isn't necessary. The professional captains and outfitters would be much better served if they accepted each animal and fish for what it is, then go and enjoy the search and successful hunt for it.

Instead, the bragging game continues. Some years ago a western hunting guide and outfitter seriously tried to impress us with the oft-repeated propaganda about the intelligence of America's fastest four-footed critter, the pronghorn antelope. This guy actually was a super-slick businessman what with him charging five of us each a $100 trespass fee on land we later discovered was federal grazing land. Get the hang of this! We paid $500 to hunt and/or trespass on land that belonged not to him, but to our Uncle Sam. And that's not talking about the money he received in addition to the trespass fees.

This Wyoming outfitter told us, "Remember, when you see an antelope inside a fence, it'll stay there and never, never will attempt to jump over it. It might run alongside the fence or cross the property to the other side where you can't get to it, but it'll never jump the fence."

The first five or six antelopes we spotted while the outfitter was back in camp — probably counting his money — approached a four-foot-high barbed wire fence at a full gallop, jumped over it, and never looked back. Another 12 or so antelopes got down on their bellies, literally, and crawled under it. So much for the never-jump-a-fence wisdom.

Next, our outfitter related that an antelope had eyesight that could favorably be compared to an 8-power binocular. "These dang things," said the oil well-owning, airplane-flying cowboy, "can see you bat an eyelash 150 yards away. They're so spooky, you'll need to crawl on your belly to get within 400 yards of them if the wind is right and even then you'd better make sure you have plenty of cover between you and the pronghorn."

The first antelope we shot was a buck with 14-inch horns (not bad, but not a record either) that practically trotted into our little campsite along the creek bank in the rolling grasslands near Gillette. The next antelope buck didn't start moving until we walked within 50 yards of him. He was so easy to shoot it was almost a pity. So it went with all the Wyoming antelopes we got during that "memorable" hunt for America's "smartest, sharpest-eyed, fastest-running, never-jumps-a-fence" wild game.

And here's another thing about the antelopes from the west. After we shot our first one and after hearing our "host" tell us how great a pronghorn's meat was, we decided to drive into town and purchase a bonus "doe stamp" so we could really load up the coolers with plenty of game. The clerk in the hardware store where licenses were sold looked at us rather strangely, asking us why we wanted another antelope. "To eat, of course," we answered. "Well, heck," said the counter man. "Hereabouts, when we want something to eat that really tastes good, we hope to shoot us an elk. Dang antelopes ain't nothin' but goats. They taste like rotten sagebrush. Ain't fit for anything else but pot roasts, and even then you have to add flavoring to overcome the sagey taste."

Guess what? The hardware store clerk was right.

So it went with the "incredibly sharp-eyed, highly intelligent" western game known as the pronghorn antelope. If the truth be known, after hunting not-too-bright mule deer a couple of times and going after "wily" Alaskan high country caribous, we're firmly convinced that a black bear or a whitetailed deer that lives in dense East Coast swamp lands or thick Eastern mountain forests is unquestionably the toughest-to-hunt game in North America, save perhaps for the great Alaskan tundra grizzly or a coastal brown bear — both of which actually belong to the same biological family, although the brown bear, or Kodiak, grows much larger. We'll readily admit that few things on earth are as tough, brazen, and dangerous as a grizzly.

Meanwhile, as far as certain fishing and hunting guides are concerned, take along a notebook and pencil and quietly write down all the great advice these veritable fountains of knowledge will smother you with. Who knows, maybe one day you can use the stuff to spruce up an otherwise dull day. One thing is certain, you'll be sure to hear some real lulus!

WHEN NOT TO WORRY ABOUT THE RAIN

If it's rainy and windy while you're fishing from your boat and you're concerned about being wet, don't be. Here's rock-solid advice you'll cherish for the rest of your life: Start your outboard and run up and down the river or lake until you're dry. The wind, you'll see, gets rid of the water. You don't even need a raincoat. When you feel that the wind has dried you up enough to let you continue fishing, go ahead. Later, if you again feel uncomfortably wet, put the throttle down and repeat the aforementioned. But if you run out of gas don't call us for advice. Just start paddling and hope the launch ramp isn't far away.

CHAPTER 2

If You Can't Join 'em, Lick 'em

THE YUPPIE COON HUNTING CLUB

Eugene's eyes aren't as good as they used to be and he'd be the first to admit that on occasion there'll be little mixups because of increasingly diminished vision when objects are near. Far off in the distance, Eugene can see just fine. In fact, his nephew, Conan, believes his uncle can hit a fly with a rifle bullet from 200 yards away as the insect sits on the edge of a bowl filled with grits — without ever disturbing the grits. That boy is definitely going to be the major benefactor of Eugene's last will and testament — if Eugene ever goes, which some folks doubt. But what happened the other day, even Conan will have a tough time understanding.

Eugene drove along a highway not far from his home when he noticed a yellow road sign that he later discovered said, "Commuting Information. Call 1-800-211-1111."

The trouble with Eugene is that he believed the sign said, "Coon hunting Information. Call 1-800-211-1111," and Eugene was truly impressed. Imagine, coon hunting information being touted on a state road sign. Now that's the way taxpayer dollars should be spent, he thought. He was delighted. He called the toll-free number and a recording of a sweet-voiced lady came on. The nice woman told Eugene to be on a certain street corner any day Monday through Friday before 7 a.m.

He wrote down the address, perfectly happy with the arrangement, although he was more than a little confused with the meeting time for the coon hunt. No one down his neck of the woods hunts coons after sunrise. They do it when the sun goes down. But what the heck, Eugene figured anybody who had enough influence to put up road signs along a highway that advertised coon hunting, probably also had enough influence to change the local hunting laws.

By 6 in the morning Eugene was dressed in his hunting clothes and wading boots and he opened the kennel door where General Lee, his bluetick hound, spends his days. "We're goin' coon hunting," he told the dog and General Lee looked at Eugene as if he'd lost his marbles. He knew that people and dogs aren't supposed to be coon hunting as the sun started to rise. Still, he willingly came along because he loves to ride in a pickup truck.

When Eugene arrived at the place the lady on the recording told him about he saw a dozen or so people already waiting. Most of them wore Sunday suits and ties and carried briefcases. General Lee looked at Eugene and shook his head. He'd never seen such well-dressed hunters — and neither had Eugene.

Then General Lee walked over to the spiffy-looking coon hunters and cocked his leg on a briefcase that one of the guys held in his hand. You should've heard the hollering and carrying-on by these people. Eugene and General Lee have seen Bantam chickens that acted more orderly.

They told Eugene to get the heck out of there and never come back. "And while you're at it," shouted the guy with the dripping leather brief case, "take your mangy mutt with you." General Lee growled at the man, which he rarely does, but then turned and left with his master.

What an odd feeling Eugene now had in the pit of his stomach. He showed up to join a new coon hunting club and got kicked out before he paid the first dollar in membership dues.

Oh well, thought Eugene, who wants to hunt coon with a bunch of daytime-lovin' Yuppies anyhow? General Lee agreed. He nodded his head, curled up on the front seat of the pickup and promptly fell asleep, probably dreaming about a pretty girl poodle that lives down the street.

NOT ALL JUMPERS ARE HORSES

You can count on two things when you spend a day with one of America's best-known bass fishermen, Roland Martin. You won't fall asleep from boredom, and people will recognize the blond fishing magician everywhere he goes.

But there's also a price to pay for sitting in the same boat with the famous Marylander who now lives in Clewiston, Fla., because the odds are better than even you'll age beyond your years before the day has ended.

For example, during a fishing tournament in the Atchafalaya Swamp in Louisiana a number of years ago, Martin had a press observer, a fellow Marylander, in the boat with him and the fishing pro wasted little time scaring the bejeebers out of his boat mate.

Martin left the docks at the start of the tournament along with the rest of the competitors, but while the others ran straight down the Atchafalaya River, keeping safely within the bounds of deep channel water, Martin suddenly cut sharply to the left and entered a flooded forest.

Have you ever driven through a forest in a bass boat?

Martin apparently bothered to check with the locals the day before and he learned that because of recent flooding from the nearby Mississippi River, there now was at least four feet of water surrounding a million cypress and other swamp land trees. Between the trees and broken-off stumps, there were crayfish traps and thousands of dense little bushes.

Do you know what likes dense little bushes when the sun shines and a warm, early morning beckons? Cottonmouth snakes, that's who!

And here Martin ran through the shrubbery, not caring one little bit about his passenger who now saw two and three fat water moccasins on just about every branch in a swamp that is the unquestionable number one world champion sanctuary for cottonmouth snakes.

"What do I do if one of these ugly cottonmouths falls into the boat?" asked Martin's partner while the fishing pro zig-zagged through the flooded timber trying to reach a deepwater bayou he's seen on a map the night before. "Make sure it doesn't get into our sandwiches, or better yet, make damned sure it doesn't start drinking our sodas because it's gonna be hotter than hades today. We need them for ourselves. To heck with the snake."

It was vintage Roland Martin, but not nearly as vintage as the BASS Masters Super Stars tournament he qualified for in 1993 and then tried to win tens of thousands of dollars on a tough, mud-stained Illinois River near Peoria.

As fate would have it the same Marylander who aged 30 years in the company of Martin during the Atchafalaya outing now was with him on the Illinois River. "I haven't seen any real bass-productive water along the main river, which really is too muddy and fast to suit me," cautioned Martin, "so I'm going to try and fish in one of those little oxbow lakes downstream."

He found such a protected river pocket behind an earthen dike maybe 35 miles from Peoria. As he entered a long canal and rounded a section of flooded willows, there it was: A large, clear-water pond that was ringed by a grass-and-dirt levee.

Martin slowed down the boat and started stashing away rods and reels and tackle boxes.

He wouldn't? He wasn't thinking of. . . ?

That's precisely what he was going to do. He said, "Don't worry about anything. I've done this before. Just hold on somewhere."

Then the 53-year-old fishing legend and TV star put the transmission of the 150-h.p. outboard motor into forward, pushed down on the throttle, picking up speed as he charged toward the narrow strip of land and ran up and over the dike at a speed of 100 m.p.h. Okay, so it wasn't 100 m.p.h., but it seemed that fast.

"Varrrrooom," screamed the Evinrude as it entered the Twilight Zone. Then it was over. Roland Martin had taken a $25,000 bass boat and jumped over a levee as if his real name was Evel Knievel.

"Now admit it," asked Martin, "it wasn't all that bad, was it?"

"Well, no, actually," was the answer. "But tell me, how are we going to get back to where we came from? Not back across the dike? You're going to jump that dike again, aren't you, only this time you'll do it from the other side?"

"How else can we run back upriver in time to eat dinner," Martin said with a laugh. "You worry too much!"

That's it. Too much worrying. It'll make your hair fall out.

THE STRANGEST DOG BREEDS OF ALL TIME

Our friends Grover Clark and Grandmother Tucker (actually it's John Tucker, but when his daughter gave birth to her first child, John's friends instantly began to refer to him as Grandmother Tucker) know a great deal about various dog breeds. Oh, we're not talking about simple breeds like a Bedlington or an Affenpinscher, no, we're talking about complicated critters that no longer exist — extinct dog breeds that Grover and Grandmother Tucker used to swear they'd seen do their work.

For example, have you ever heard of an oyster pointer? We thought so. You haven't, have you?

At any rate, Grover and Grandmother Tucker used to talk about them being fairly plentiful. "The oyster pointer was a wonderful animal," they'd recall. "They'd wait until the tide ran low along the shores of the Chesapeake Bay, and these great dogs would run out onto the tidal flats and pick up the scent of delectable oysters. Bang! They'd lock into a rigid point as pretty as any dog has ever pointed a quail or a pheasant.

"Sadly, a lot of times when these marvelous dogs were locked into pointing the oysters, their human masters weren't around. So the dogs held their point, never wavering for one minute. Well, the tide eventually would begin to flow again and get high and the dogs would drown.

"It happened so often around the Bay area that eventually the breed became very rare. Some dog owners would cross-breed them with other pointers, but it never worked out very well. Today, you don't see these fine oyster pointers any longer. They're gone — a sad reminder of a once proud breed of hunting dog."

Then Grover and Grandmother Tucker would quickly walk away, wiping their eyes along the way. They obviously didn't want anybody to see them become so emotional.

The Clam Beagles

Jack White, who was raised in Massachusetts and now lives in Maine (or one of those states where they eat moose nose stew and live so close to Canada the natives finish every sentence with "eh?") once told us about an odd breed of dog he saw along Cape Cod or Cuttyhunk, Mass.

"I spotted two dogs, black and white and brown in color, run along the shoreline like bats from hell, yowling and yipping just as if they were hot on the trail of a cottontail rabbit. Suddenly, they'd stop and run in circles, nose to the ground, then start scratching like mad.

"Before you knew it, they'd scratched up a bunch of hardshelled clams, one of them even carried the clams — one at a time — down to the ocean's edge and kind of let the onrushing water run through his mouth, washing off the sand the clams were covered with. Then the two clam beagles took the bivalves up to the dune grass where their master put them into a pail to be taken home and steamed."

Jack was asked whatever happened to the clam beagle breed.

"Strange thing," Jack answered. "It appears the various braces of beagles would frequently get so engrossed in their digging chores, the tide would begin to rush in, surprise them and drown them. "I don't think there are any left today," Jack said.

Well, if you're getting the kind of feeling that this is deja vu all over again, as the great English language professor Yogi Berra once remarked when something recurred, just look at the oyster pointer saga. There you have it!

The Trout Retriever

Howard Holliday, a dear friend and native son of West Virginia, once told us about a little dog his wife had picked up for $2 at a county dog pound. "It has a flat face and is ugly as a toady frog," he pointed out, "but it likes water. I can't keep that little sucker from running into my kid's wading pool."

Howard, who never told a fib and kind of expected others to be as honest with him as he always was, looked a little bewildered when we told him what he had on his hands was not a pug or a Pekinese dog, but a rare and probably very expensive trout retriever.

"A what? A trout retriever?" Howard asked incredulously.

"That's right, Howard, a trout retriever," we'd answer, then explain that long ago in central Europe where the fishing for brown trout has turned into a fine art over the centuries, a smart breeder trained a dog to jump into a stream and snatch a resting brown trout right off a flat rock before the fish knew what happened.

"Unfortunately, Howard, the dogs over the years would sometimes mis-judge the precise location of the trout and slam their once-pointed muzzles smack dab on top of the rocks. Well, you can imagine, Howard, over time, with each succeeding generation the dogs' noses receded and now look at 'em. They don't have much of a face, do they?"

"You'd best not be messin' with me," Howard said, "because I'm goin' home and I'll be tellin' my family that we have a truly famous dog breed in our house. And if you lied to me, your butts will be grass and I'll be the lawn mower."

Fortunately, Howard moved out of the state before he had a chance to catch up with us. But anytime we see a stocky, well-built man with a full head of silver-hued hair, we go the other way. We just don't know whether any member of his family had the guts to laugh at him and he in turn now was mad at us, but we're not taking any chances.

SPARKLE-BOATS DO STRANGE THINGS TO GROWN MEN

Put a person into an aluminum johnboat or an old wooden rowboat and chances are he or she will remain perfectly normal people who enjoy the nibble from a fish. And if the fish decide not to cooperate, so be it.

All that goes out the window when a 20th Century phenomenon occurs that brave souls everywhere recognize as the "bass boat."

A bass boat can be used for any purpose, save perhaps for ocean travel, but when certain human beings take a seat at the steering wheel or on the pro-throne seat near where the electric trolling motor pedal is located, a transformation takes place that is nothing less than astonishing. Otherwise good people suddenly turn into ogres. Quiet, meek individuals become loud-mouthed jerks. Below-average fishermen take on the mannerisms of super pro anglers who follow the touring circuit of the Bass Anglers Sportsman Society.

It happens so regularly that it's becoming a standing joke among those who can handle the glistening sparkle of the metal-flake paint jobs, or the sudden response from a 150-h.p. outboard. But those who can't cope with being in a modern sparkle-boat are outnumbering those who can.

Just the other day, we sat near the outflow channel of a large electric plant, hoping to catch a tidal river striper. Another boat sat nearby, its two occupants casting lures rapidly, never saying a word. Their casting intensified even more when a large rockfish suddenly struck one of our rattle lures and the fight with the fish became clearly visible as it neared the surface and we readied a landing net to capture it.

The striper weighed around 15 or 16 pounds. It thrashed the river surface, kicking butt, testing our fishing line's strength with every flip and roll. The two men who sat nearby watched, mouths sagging, then suddenly, inexplicably they reeled in their lines and departed. Why they left when it was plain that there would be some kind of fishing action in the waters they were in, is difficult to explain unless the "bass boat" factor is taken into account.

You see, it could be the duo couldn't accept the fact that someone else hooked a fish right before their eyes while they couldn't catch a cold.

Later, when we returned to the ramp the two men had just finished loading their boat onto a trailer and the nearest one to us, when asked whether they'd ever done any good after they left the vicinity we met in, said with anguish, "Not a fish. Nothing."

Meanwhile, the other man, not knowing what his partner had told us, was asked in the snack shop some 10 minutes later how he fared. "Hmmpphh," he snorted. "We limited out 10 minutes after we left you guys. Hmmpppphh! Shucks, we were cullin' fish the rest of the morning. This place is overrun with rockfish."

He obviously didn't know what his pal had just told us. "Hmmpphh! Indeed!"

And last week, when we returned from another trip and tied the boat to a dock to let another angler finish putting his craft on a trailer, we eventually asked him how he'd done. "Man, I tell you, this place is so loaded with lunkers, I can't believe it. I hooked 65 rockfish this morning alone. Where did I catch 'em? On the Hawks Nest buoy out on the river, do you know it?"

We did, indeed. Only we didn't have the nerve to tell him that we, too, sat in the waters around the Hawks Nest buoy — and we didn't see another boat there all day long. The reason we stayed there so long is because when we arrived at daybreak we hooked two fat stripers almost immediately, then fiddled around, casting, talking, not doing much of anything, waiting for the tide to turn, knowing the action might get better.

It just goes to show that if you're going to tell tall stories, get together with your partner to coordinate what it is you're going to say. And if you're going to hook 65 good fish in one spot, don't pick a well-known place visited by others. Choose a place so vague and out-of-the-way that nobody actually knows where you were.

Finally, if you own a sparkle-boat and you believe

you're the King Kong of all the great bass fishermen and you're ready to leave your family to pursue a big-bucks professional fishing career, don't do it. For every super bass angler who thinks he's the best, there are actually three others hiding in the hinterlands who will whip your tail so bad, there won't be much left to tuck between your legs when you run away.

Bob and Gene recommend that you just enjoy your fishing and leave it at that. And, please, whenever you go fishing and the kids are home and don't have to go to school, take one or two with you. Children love to fish and until they discover dating, kissing and stuff like that you might as well teach them how to catch dinner.

DUCK, BILL, DUCK!

Our friend Jack Moore, born and raised on the Eastern Shore of Maryland and proud of it, loves to hunt ducks. Jack, in fact, likes to hunt ducks a lot more than geese, which is saying something since one Canada goose or one snow goose can feed four people, while four ducks would have a tough time feeding one human with an appetite.

At any rate, Jack sometimes goes after the "good eating" ducks, as he refers to mallards, blacks and woodies, in an aluminum boat that is push-poled along the edge of a river. There is no motor, only a long wooden pole that is held by one hunter who stands on the bench seat nearest the stern of the boat, while another hunter sits in the middle doing nothing, and a shooter who stands — legs spread and braced against the insides of the gunwales — in the bow, shotgun at the ready, waiting for a couple of greenheads to burst from the water as they spot the approaching boat.

If the boat is close enough — say, less than 50 yards — the shooter in the bow takes a crack at the waterfowl. When he's done, the man in the middle takes the bow stand, and so on until the trio has a legal limit of ducks.

Well, the day came when Bill Walls, as hardy and tough an Eastern Shore native as you're likely to meet, joined Moore and another stout fellow for a push-poling day of duck hunting on the upper Chester River in Kent County. By the flip of a coin it was decided that Bill would be first in the bow, while Jack sat in the middle and the third man did the poling. You understand, of course, the reason that the boys didn't use an outboard motor for this was the fact that it was illegal to hunt with a motor-propelled boat. You weren't even allowed to have a loaded gun inside a motor boat that was running along.

Bill took his place, a shotgun held across his chest, while the boat silently slid along the densely tree-lined shore of the Chester River. Then it happened.

"Duck, Bill, duck!" Jack Moore whispered suddenly and as loudly as he dared. Bill looked around sharply, hissing, "Where are they?" Just then a low-hanging branch from a large sycamore tree slapped Bill alongside his head so hard it knocked him clear out of the boat and into the river.

Mind you now, it was January and the time for taking a dip in the Chester was not now. Bill disappeared in the bubbling tidal water, then resurfaced like a wet golden retriever, his gun still firmly in his hand, and he simply said, "Oh, you mean that kind of duck."

With that the Eastern Shore hunter pulled himself into the boat and only motioned for one of the other men to take the bow. "I think I'll push-pole the boat the rest of the day," he said. "The exercise will keep me warm."

Bill knew that his country boy pals weren't about to go home just because one member of the party got soaked. Since the day had just started he also knew they were still a dozen ducks shy of a limit.

SOMETIMES IT'S SMART TO BE DUMB

He can only be identified as Johnson, which actually isn't his monicker, but it will do.

Johnson, you see, is one of those fishermen who doesn't believe in carrying his share of the load. When it's time to drop the old johnboat from the back of a pickup into a lake and you look around for a helping hand, Johnson is nowhere to be seen. So you do it all alone, risking a hernia, and the moment you finish Johnson comes from around the corner adjusting the zipper on his fly.

"Oh, did you have to pull the boat out all by yourself?" he'll ask innocently. "Yeah, I had to," you answer in a slightly irritated voice and he'll shamelessly mumble something about how you should have shouted for him when there was a job to be done.

Soon enough it's time to stash one or two super-heavy trolling motor batteries into the boat, not to mention oars, tackle boxes and a cooler. Please, understand that some of the batteries are heavy enough to make Hulk Hogan break into a sweat, so maybe it's understandable that Johnson suddenly remembers an old back injury and how the doctor told him not to lift anything heavier than a doughnut or a hoagie.

When the boat's loaded Johnson apparently has enough strength to climb into it, but say one thing about a new knot you've read about and he'll instantly come back with, "I was just going to bring up that new knot. In fact, I'd like to show you a shortcut when tying it, but I can't bend my finger real good. I cut it this morning and it's real sore. If my finger were okay I could give a seminar on this kind of knot tying."

So you do the knots and you land the fish and you bring the sandwiches (because his finger is sore) and in the end you can say only one thing: "Sometimes it's smart to be dumb because when you play dumb you don't have to do any of the work; somebody else will do it for you."

Here's betting there's a Johnson in your circle of fishing acquaintances.

COPS KNOW NOTHING ABOUT RUNAWAY DOGS

Our friend Danny McCuiston owned a fine coon dog, a bluetick hound he paid plenty of money for. So it'll come as no surprise that Danny was more than a little chagrined when he returned from his job one night and discovered his dog was gone.

Danny called the police to report a stolen coon hound. When the cops arrived they questioned Danny about the dog and asked how he was so sure that his hound had been stolen. "Couldn't he have run away from home just as easily?" asked one of the officers.

"There's no way my hound ran away from home," said Danny. "See that bag of dog food over there in the garage," asked Danny. "If he ran away, he'd have taken that bag of Wayne's Meal with him. No sir, he's the victim of dog-nappers, I'm telling you."

HOW TO FOOL SQUIRRELS

Over the decades, it has always amazed us how a relatively small furbearer like a squirrel manages to make a fool of grown hunters. Fear not, however. Bob and Gene to the rescue: When you enter the woods for a squirrel hunt, put your cap on backwards. In other words, let the bill of the hat hang over your neck the way some youngsters look these days when they come to school. When the squirrel sees you with the backward cap, it'll think you're leaving the woods instead of coming in and it'll run around the tree limbs as if everything was fine. Go ahead and get your limit and don't thank us. We're glad to pass this along.

CHAPTER 3

Good Food is More Important Than Fishing and Hunting

NEVER LET A SKINNY GUY MAKE SANDWICHES

Be truthful now, if you're about to spend a day on the water or in the woods (or in a city park, for that matter) and two distinctly different types of people offer to bring the sandwiches, which one would you pick? Would you choose a skinny acquaintance who likes to jog and who is definitely into health foods, or would you pick a corpulent pal who loves to cook pots full of Louisiana gumbo for his friends? You know the answer. It's the person who knows the difference between mambo and gumbo. (Mambo you dance; gumbo you eat.)

When we plan a day-long fishing trip or hunt in an area that does not have a ready supply of food stores or restaurants, the fixing of the sandwiches is as important as the most sought-after quarry. Food, after all, is something you can't do without. Yes, we realize that there are people who eat to live, as well as people who live to eat. Rest assured that Bob and Gene belong to the latter group.

"Imagine," a friend said recently, "being caught hundreds of miles from home with sandwiches so thin that a body could read a newspaper through them?" Yes, we can imagine it. In fact, we've met people who believed that sustenance could be gained from two pieces of wafer-thin, square, white bread that is wrapped around a soggy lettuce leaf and one thin, square slice of bologna that, oddly, has the same dimensions as the bread slices.

That's the trouble with everyday, lousy, inedible sandwiches: Nothing pokes out from the sides. The people who make them are actually proud that everything fits without the slightest overhang, so we'd like to hang those who believe that drivel, just as we'd like to drown the ad man who convinced the Budweiser beer people to let him brag about the fact that Budweiser uses rice in its beer. For shame, here's betting every German brew master who's ever drawn a Stein of beer from an oak barrel, but now has departed this earth, is spinning in his grave.

Now, back to the sandwiches. Here's the way to make one you'll never hear a complaint about: Start with a foot-long section of bakery-fresh Italian or French bread. Fresh, crusty German or Jewish rye bread will also do, but we recommend it only if it's cut from a whole loaf bought in a bakery. Forget the cellophane-wrapped packages it's usually sold in.

To continue the sandwich preparation, spread good mayonnaise on one side of the bread, high-quality Dijon mustard on the other. Distribute half a pound of super-thin baked ham slices loosely all over the bread. Let it hang out over the sides in no particular order. Add eight or nine thin slices of Italian salami. Scatter pickled pepper rings across the sandwich, but be sure to shake excess pickling liquid from the peppers so the bread won't become soggy. Add very thin slices of Bermuda onion, then drop a few slices of turkey breast, thin Swiss cheese, and six or seven bread-and-butter pickle chips over the onions. Fold the top layer of bread over this joyous collection of goodies and take a big bite by holding the sandwich firmly in both hands. You must make sure that nothing falls out.

Well, what's the verdict? Terrific, eh?

Sorry about saying "eh" in the paragraph above. The "eh" sound is one that is typically uttered by Canadians, particularly those from Ontario. Right here and now, let us tell you if you should plan a trip to Canada, take along a bunch of the sandwiches we've given you the recipe for. A large percentage of Canadians is closely related to the English and everybody knows that in England good food is as tough to come by as laws that say you can drive on the right-hand side of the street.

The Canadians, for some strange reason — and despite them having lots of beef, plenty of land, seafood, and wild game to spare — have never quite gotten the hang of learning how to cook good food. God bless our neighbors to the north, but all the same, take all the fixings for however many sandwiches you think you'll need if you visit English-speaking Canada. However, if Quebec is on the itinerary, relax. The French-Canadians eat well — very well.

Meanwhile, if you spend your days in the U.S. and

good food becomes an important part of your time spent outdoors, do it in the Southern states. New England, for example, isn't known for knock-your-socks-off great food. It probably has something to do with the second part of the name New England. But if you're "stranded" on fishing waters anywhere from Southern Maryland to Florida, as well as from Tennessee to Texas, we can assure that you'll never be far away from good vittles. Translate the word vittles into meaning barbecue.

As anybody with any sense knows, barbecue is the staff of life! Okay, if you don't have good sense, we'll help out and provide an easy primer for fishermen and hunters and plain nature lovers who'll find themselves in the not-soon-to-be-forgotten Dixieland.

In the lower section of Maryland (it used to be a hotbed for Confederates during the Civil War) you'll find barbecue shacks in Charles County that'll sell a hungry soul succulent pork ribs and barbecued pork chops. Rather than call a large section of ribs a "rack," as Yankees would, the Charles Countians refer to it as a "slab." Bring your appetite or do some serious training if you believe you can eat a whole "slab." Wow!

In Virginia, you're apt to find ribs, chops and barbecued chicken. The barbecue will almost always be of the sweet variety, kind of like the world-renowned Memphis barbecue. Then you'll head into North and South Carolina and quickly become used to a vinegar-based chopped pork barbecue, which then is complemented with tangy, sweet barbecued chicken and pork chops from South Carolina to Florida. Talk about your taste buds doing a happy two-step — this is it.

Texans have delectable barbecued brisket that has been rubbed with dry seasoning and cooked slowly over wood coals, then is sliced and sauced as it's heaped onto your plate. Don't overlook the sausages that are grilled and are as Texan as a cowboy hat. Our good friend Bill Garner, who is a Texan, although he roots for the Redskins rather than the Dallas Cowboys, says the area around Austin is particularly good for those who want to dive into real good Texas barbecued brisket and sausage.

What we're getting at is that in the United States it's the Southerners and Southern food sympathizers who would probably rather drown in a muddy lake than eat soggy bologna sandwiches.

SAUSAGE GRAVY IS BETTER THAN WHEAT GERM

A long-time acquaintance of ours has been pestering us for years to take him fishing. Well, he finally got his wish when we couldn't take his whining any longer. It's not that we didn't want to go fishing with him — he's a nice enough fellow — it's just that it's so darned tough to break in new fishing companions who'll want you to listen to their political beliefs, sometimes even want you to come to church with them, and just generally are more trouble than they're worth.

But we agreed to do it all the same, even though we were filled with a great deal of apprehension. Our feelings served us well because — scout's honor — this guy shows up wearing one of those silly looking up-downer hats. Do you know the kind? It greatly resembles the hats mothers put on their babies when they take them outside in a stroller. It has a bill poking out in front to shade the face and another one coming out the back to — we suppose — shade the collar of a jacket or shirt. Personally, we've never owned jackets and shirts that wanted to be shaded, but different strokes for different folks.

Are we making sense so far?

Well, this man in his red up-downer baby stroller hat arrives at the prearranged meeting site in a foreign car, which didn't set well with us because we're heavy into buying American. But that wasn't a big problem when compared to the wicker picnic basket he pulled from the little puddle-jumper's backseat. "Whatcha got in the basket?" was the immediate question. "Lunch," he said, which sounded pretty good. We're always ready for lunch — even when it's only 5 a.m.

But all our enthusiasm for the food disappeared quickly when we sneaked a look in the basket and there — and we weren't all that surprised by it — was a cheap bottle of white wine (it had a screw-on cap which means it's cheap, doesn't it?) and a plain loaf of French bread. "Where's the meat," we practically screamed at the poor baby hat wearer. "There is no meat," he answered sheepishly. "But I did bring a wedge of Brie cheese and some watercress."

We'll say no more about the rest of the day, save, perhaps, to serve notice that anyone who feels about food the way this Yuppie does, will never be invited to come fishing with us. Enough said?

Real men and women don't eat watercress, folks. Real people have slices of homemade bread with sausage gravy for breakfast, maybe a bowl full of deer meat chili for lunch, and barbecued ribs or a T-bone steak for dinner. Oh, sure, you're allowed to substitute other foods, but the aforementioned dishes will be a kind of starter set for you so you'll have an idea where all this is headed.

In the Denyer household, sausage gravy has been developed into an art form. There isn't a family friend anywhere who will not answer the call to come for breakfast at the Denyer house. You'll see a gallon of smooth, white milk gravy, just thick enough to keep from running off the plate, and so crammed full with chunks of nicely-seasoned pork sausage you sometimes wonder if the family didn't grind up a whole hog just to make gravy for one morning session.

Then there'll be eggs, sunny-side up or over-easy, by the dozen. And buttered bread with pots full of coffee and orange juice. By the time you finish breakfast you won't care whether the fish will bite or a duck will come into the decoys because you're so happy, you just don't have time to become grumpy about anything.

As far as good advice is concerned for folks who worry about eating health foods, we have oodles of it and it's all free of charge (if you don't count the price of this book).

For example, tofu, that white, watery brick of squeezed, bleached soybean that can be purchased in most grocery stores is great for filling cracks in your sidewalk. Use a putty knife and wedge it into the cracks, then allow a few days to let it dry. Don't worry about anything bothering the tofu. It won't happen. Even ants stay away from that stuff, although we once saw a dog cock his leg on some of it.

And what about wheat germ? Doctors say it's a good source of fiber and has all sorts of beneficial things in it. Don't believe it. It's a massive conspiracy by the nation's cereal companies. Just like all packaged cereals it tastes exactly like cardboard, only it's granulated. Regular corn flakes are more like chips of cardboard. Don't eat either one. Instead, put it out in the garage or the basement where mice have been a problem. Once the mice find out that's all they're going to get, they'll leave and head for your neighbor's house.

If you want fiber and good taste, eat two or three crisp apples. You'll be as regular as a commuter railroad.

Watercress, by the way, is ideal rabbit food. If you don't have rabbits, try and get one from a farm supply house or a breeder. Feed the rabbit the watercress mixed with some alfalfa pellets and it'll grow big and sassy. Then, when you feel like it, butcher the rabbit and stew, fry, or bake it. Either way, it'll be a lot tastier than watercress. If you can't bring yourself to kill the rabbit, call us, we'll do it. It'll cost you half the animal, however, because we don't butcher anything for free.

Then there's yogurt. You, of course, know that yogurt is actually one, big, massive bacteria. Just take a look at the carton it comes in and you'll immediately be warned to keep it covered and refrigerated. Do you know why? We do. We once saw a horror movie where a cup of yogurt was left out on the kitchen counter. During the night, it grew and grew like the Blob. It eventually ate the whole family, the dog, and the house. Only an attack with nuclear-tipped artillery shells by the U.S. Army was finally able to kill the thing off. That's yogurt. Do you still want some? We didn't think so.

Don't get us wrong when we put down certain "health" foods. We don't mind health food when it comes in the form of a great, big mixed salad made of lettuce, spinach, carrots, tomatoes, green peppers and onions. In fact, we love it — if it also has a spicy Italian dressing and maybe a couple handsful of diced ham and chicken. And we're fully aware of the worth of legumes — beans belong to the group, all you country folks. We love beans, especially in a chili filled with pounds and pounds of ground venison and lots of tomatoes, garlic and onions.

Now, that's health food anybody can live with.

MOONSHINE ISN'T ALWAYS A LUNAR CONDITION

Not long ago on a Tennessee highway a state policeman who'd been on the force less than a year, spotted a pickup truck whose tires looked flat from all the weight that pressed down on them. Over the bed of the truck, a large green tarp covered a huge mound of some unknown substance. The tarp was tied down with bungee cords that strained and wiggled with every bump the truck drove over.

The highway patrolman decided to stop the vehicle. The driver, a native Kentuckian who answered to the name Danny, slowly stopped. "Dang it all," Danny thought to himself. "If only I could've driven another two miles, I'da been home in Kentucky and wouldn't have to put up with this young pup."

"What are you carryin' in the truck, mister?" asked the rookie trooper who'd spent most of his years in Memphis, not in the hills near the Kentucky border. "Sugar, Cap'n," answered Danny, "sugar."

"My Lord," said the policeman, "that's an awful lot of sugar to be carrying in such a small pickup truck. Heck, it's about to break the rear springs."

"Yeah, I know, Cap'n," said Danny. "But what are you goin' to do when your mom tells you to go to town and buy her a bunch of sugar so she can put up peaches? Maybe you argue with your mother, but I don't with mine 'cause she's got a mean temper. Besides, her peaches are truly fine. I'll have to put a couple of jars of 'em in the truck. Next time I see you, I'll let you taste 'em."

With that the Kentuckian drove on to his home on the other side of the border. The trooper sat there for a while, then radioed his station commander. "Lieutenant," he began, "is it possible for anybody to need a whole truck filled with sugar if they want to can peaches?"

"In January?" asked the incredulous veteran cop. "No way."

By then, of course, it was too late to catch up with Danny. He was up in the woods, far away, delivering the staff of life that is required to turn corn into corn squeezin's.

Moonshine, you understand, isn't just a lunar condition that makes hound dogs howl and young boys wish they were with young girls. If "cooked" properly and without taking dangerous shortcuts, it's the elixir that has delighted many a mountain man.

This recalls an incident back in Clarke County, Va., when a local boy and a visitor from the city decided to take a shortcut through a dense woodland to reach a well-hidden section of a Blue Ridge Mountains trout stream. The country-wise woodsman warned his new-found city-bred friend to pay strict attention to strange smells, sudden whisps of smoke, odd noises and anything else that seemed out-of-place.

"What are you talking about?" asked the man from Washington, who, to be perfectly fair, spent more time in a high-rise office than in the Blue Ridge country of Virginia. "I'm talking about moonshine stills and the people who make it. They won't take kindly to a stranger walking up on their still, especially one who might carry a Washington, D.C. driver's license. They worry about 'revenoors' as Snuffy Smith calls 'em in the comic strips."

"Get out of here," said the city boy. "Moonshine stills? Come on. They don't still make moonshine, do they?"

The question had barely been finished when the city fellow, a BMW-driving Yuppie of the first order, crashed through a hole in the ground and started screaming for help when he disappeared in what appeared to be a huge, empty barrel that had been buried, its top rim even with the ground. With a thin wooden lid and a pile of leaves covering it, you'd never have known it was there.

"I nearly broke my flyrod on this damned water barrel," said the Yuppie. "Damn it all! Why on earth would anybody way out here stick a barrel into the ground to catch rain water. A body could kill himself falling into this thing."

"Yes, why indeed," answered the country boy who pulled the city visitor from his precarious position, then quietly mumbled to himself, "It's a good thing the barrel wasn't filled with 'moon.' It probably would have killed your body and mine, too, had anybody been around to catch us."

All of which serves as a warning to woodland walkers in the high back country. There are no rain barrels buried in the middle of wilderness. Only barrels that'll hold moonshine, well-hidden and concealed, blended with the forest's ground so the 'revenoors' can't find them.

Did you hear about the one-armed angler and the fish he caught? It was t–h–a–t long!

A GOOD-TIME LEXICON FOR OUTDOORSMEN

The "dictionary" below attempts to clarify only those words and meanings that actually matter in life, hence don't expect real difficult, multi-syllable entries, such as "inexplicable" or "incredulous," For starters, we don't even know what those words mean. Besides, when you're fishing and hunting, chances are you won't need either one. However, here are some you must get to know intimately:

BACKLASH — Never having had one of these, we can only repeat what others have said. A backlash apparently is when the line on your reel travels faster than the lure, thus creating a bit of a mess. This is particularly true among those who use baitcasting reels. (Also see "Bird's Nest" and "Professional Overrun.")

BIRD'S NEST — A nice word for a "Backlash," but it's the same thing. The word "Bird's Nest" comes from the way a "Backlash" looks: Like the nest of a very messy bird.

DOVE — A huge money maker for the manufacturers of small diameter shotgun loads. A dove hunter typically averages eight shots per bird.

DEER — A split-hooved, four-stomach ruminant with an enormous appetite. A deer will eat anything that'll fit into its mouth. In that way it acts a lot like a goat.

Deer are thought to be very bright only by unsuccessful hunters and city people who show up at anti-hunt demonstrations.

HAWG — A word usually reserved for truly big largemouth bass. (Also, see "Sow.")

MAALOX — What you need when other antacids don't work. (See "Tums/Rolaids".)

POKE-RINES — Little ringlets of deep-fried pork skins. Especially tasty when dredged through cayenne pepper.

PROFESSIONAL OVERRUN — What Bob and Gene sometimes experience when they use baitcasting reels. It's a simple miscalculation that either of the boys quickly corrects — sometimes as the lure is in mid-air.

RAY SCOTT — What every bass fisherman wants to wake up as tomorrow morning. Ray Scott is the man who dreamed up the international Bass Anglers Sportsman Society, along the way inventing professional bass tournaments, and also becoming very rich in the process.

SOW — A word that is used by bass fisherman when the word "Hawg" somehow isn't descriptive enough.

TAR — Usually made from nylon or rubber. If even only one tar is flat on your vehicle, you won't be able to drive very far. If you do, it'll be a bumpy ride.

TUMS/ROLAIDS — What you need after eating peppery poke-rines. (Also see "Maalox.")

TWIG — A piece of a tree, but usually very thin. You need a twig if you want to pry a Vienna sausage from its can.

VIENNIES — Little canned sausages you would refuse to eat if your wife served them for dinner. Yet, while fishing or hunting they're thought of as delicacies. Vienna sausages are best when "cured" in a tackle box for several seasons. Warning: Don't eat if the can has bulged from the heat and now looks like a baseball. (Also see "Twig.")

WATER — A liquid that is needed by fish, car batteries and washing machines. Never drink water because fish and beavers poop in it.

WALLEYE — A strange creature that primarily lives in northern lakes and rivers. A walleye is said to be the best tasting fish found in freshwater. It fights like a wet wash rag. Don't believe anybody who indicates otherwise.

WAHOO — A shout of joy when a country boy finds a barrel of moonshine in the woods and there's no one else around. A Wahoo, according to some folks, is also a fish that lives in the ocean.

YULE — An old Southern word contraction, as in "Yule laugh like a hyena when I tell you this joke."

SURE-FIRE WAY TO CATCH TROUT THROUGH ICE

Ice-fishermen are a peculiar lot; the less said about them the better. But there are situations when it has to be done because you don't want to stay home with your wife who always finds dumb chores for you to do during winter. (Painting the living room is one of them.) Instead, go to the barn and dig around the horse manure and dirt compost pile until you have a handful of lively, wriggling worms. Visit your favorite trout stream, which now is frozen solid, and cut a hole through the ice, then walk up the stream above the ice hole and place your live worms on top of the frozen stuff. Fish can see even through ice and when they spot the wiggling mess of delicacies they'll rush up to get the snack and knock their noggins against the hard stuff. They'll be out cold and will float downstream. Simply go to your ice hole and pick them from the water.

GINGER'S RECIPE FOR TENDER VENISON

A West Virginia couple, Doug and Ginger, love to serve venison. Occasionally, however, the two bag a buck that is so chewy you couldn't get a fork through the gravy. Now that's tough, isn't it?

Ginger says to cut up the deer even if it's an old one and bone it out, then put the various cuts into several layers of Saran wrap. "Lay the deer meat into the ruts of your driveway," says Ginger, "and after you've driven over it for a week or so, it'll be as tender as the best Prime USDA beef."

You don't think Ginger is pulling our leg, do you?